how can we be sustainable?

Share

Share booklet 06

This *Share booklet* is one of a series which aims to encourage discussion about fresh expressions of church, without telling you what to do.

01 how can fresh expressions emerge?
02 how should we start?
03 what should we start?
04 how can we get support?
05 how can we find our way?
06 how can we be sustainable?
07 how can we be a great team?

Contents

What is in your DNA?	3
What does sustainability involve?	4
Sustaining the pioneer	6
Shaped for the context	7
Handing over leadership	8
Dealing with problems	10
Keeping the venture fresh	13

What is in your DNA?

How can we be sustainable? is about considering sustainability in the very early stages of a fresh expression of church, not when the venture is well underway.

The long and the short of it

This booklet does not offer you a step-by-step model but will explore how, far from being an after-thought, sustainability needs to be in the fresh expression's DNA - or basic makeup.

Sustainability includes discipleship, worship and much else. This booklet focuses on some of the organisational aspects of keeping the emerging Christian community fruitful and fresh.

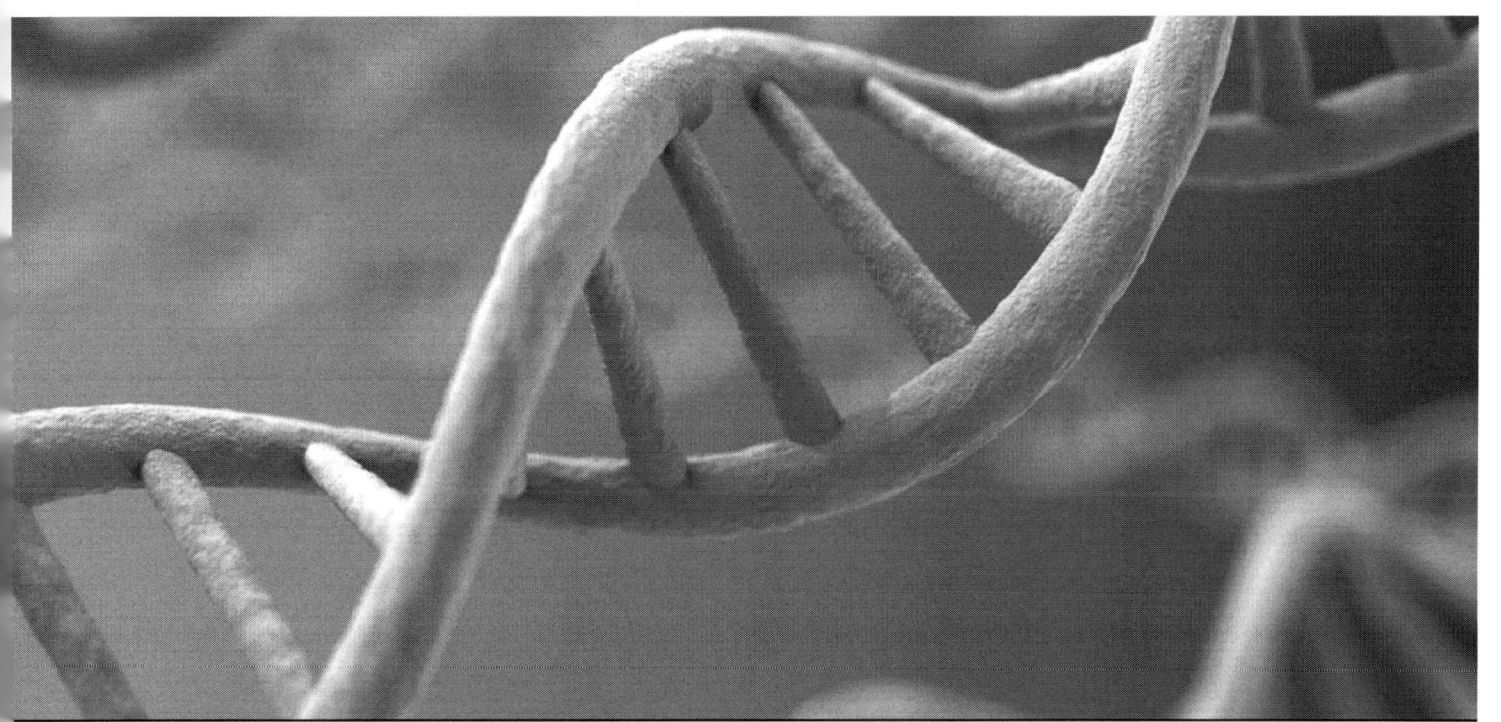

What does sustainability involve?

Are you trying to develop your fresh expression but don't know which way to turn? Take time to look at opportunities from a different angle. It can be all too easy to get stuck in a rut but a new way of thinking may lead to some radical results.

Choosing the right 'lens'

Sustainability in church planting has tended to be understood in terms of the 'three selfs', which were formulated separately by the 19th century missionary strategists, Henry Venn and Rufus Anderson. On this view, fresh expressions should become:

- **self-financing;**
- **self-governing;**
- **self-reproducing.**

There is also a fourth self that some have recently added:

- **self-theologising.**

A sustainable venture will develop a 'local theology' that responds to its context.

This 'three/four selfs' approach can hit problems if it is applied to fresh expressions through the lens of inherited church. You can end up assuming that a new church will be rather like existing churches, just as many 'daughter' churches were in the past.

The new church will become financially independent with its own minister, its own church council, its own representatives in the denominational structures and it may go on to plant a further church, which will take a similar form.

But if you apply the three/four selfs in a contextual way, you may end up thinking quite radically - more radically than has sometimes happened with fresh expressions.

A teenage congregation might interpret 'self-financing' as relying on two part-time youth workers, both of whom are financially self-supporting because they have part-time jobs.

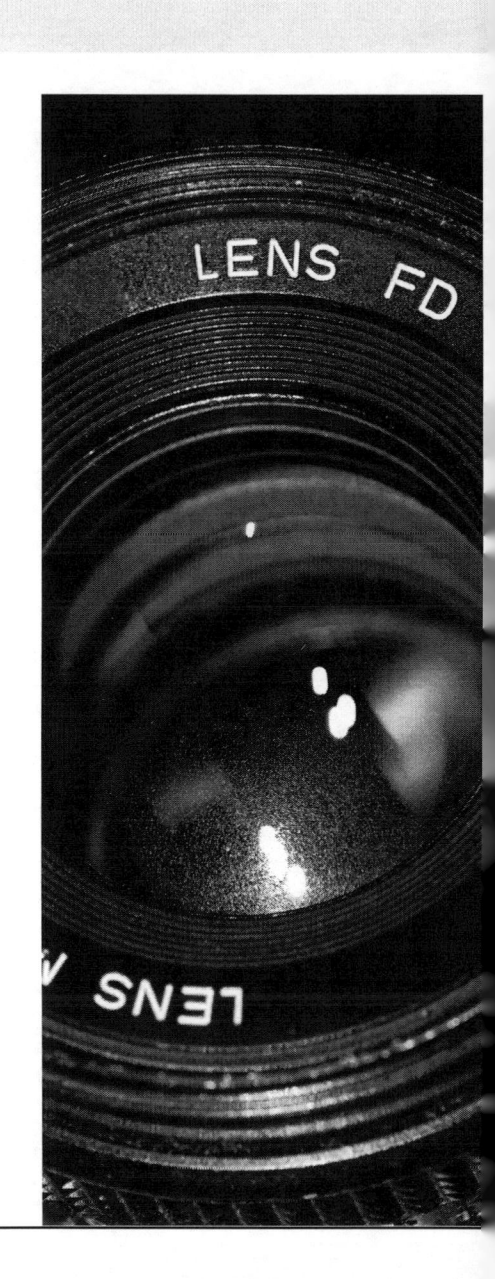

Bob Hopkins, *The 3-Self Principle - which end of the telescope?*, ACPI
tinyurl.com/acpi3self

Self-reproducing might involve new believers finding one or two other Christians in their work or their street, and starting a very small expression of church in the midst of their everyday lives.

Self-governing might be understood not as the fresh expression being independent of its parent church, but as having responsibility for its affairs within the governance structures of the local church.

Ultimately, if we are to use the three/four selfs criteria, we must think about financial sustainability, leadership and multiplication in ways that fit the context.

Despite their possibilities, the three/four selfs are still open to criticism. Do they downplay interdependence? Is the model too static for all fresh expressions?

So perhaps we should understand sustainability differently as a fresh expression. This would involve being:

- **connected to the wider church;**

    In relationships of mutual respect and support, so that the fresh expression helps to sustain the whole body and receives from it.

- **appropriately responsible;**

    The degree of financial, administrative and other responsibility will vary from one context to another and be appropriate to the context.

- **viable for its life span;**

    Some new churches will be seasonal, others longer term. The accent should be on viability while the community lasts rather than always assuming permanence.

- **attentive to flow.**

    Fresh expressions will manage the flow of their members to another Christian community, where appropriate, so that individuals have a sustained church involvement. If individuals need to change church as their spirituality evolves or circumstances change, they will be helped to do so. Sometimes sustainability will be more about flow than durability.

It will be important not to fill in these details too early to avoid prejudging what the fresh expression will be like. The meaning of 'appropriately responsible', for example, may only become apparent as the emerging church develops. We must not close down possibilities by prejudging how the Spirit will lead.

Sustaining the pioneer

Caring for the 'carers'. Spare more than a thought for the pioneer who is busy thinking of everyone else.

Whatever the size of venture, it is easy for leaders to get burnt out and put the church-start at risk. To a significant extent, the health of the Christian community will be bound up with the well-being of its leaders.

Selecting the right people is an obvious first step in sustaining pioneers, while attending to their walk with God will be pioneers' own first responsibility.

Appropriate support should be available - either arranged by the pioneer, or by the pioneering team or with the help of those to whom the pioneer is accountable.

Experience tells us that pioneers need:
- **someone to cry and laugh with;**
- **a spiritual director or companion;**
- **prayer support;**
- **appropriate training;**
- **a coach or mentor who can both listen and advise from experience;**
- **advice and support from others in a similar field;**
  Preferably from someone who has planted a fresh expression in a similar context or been involved in a comparable type of venture.
- **specialist expertise.**
  For example in finance, legal and other matters.

ENC Story

Changing from one size to another also leads to changes in how people connect with each other and those around them. In the early days of Exeter Network Church (ENC), everybody used to pitch in and do everything together - now it's too big to even know everyone.

Started in 2005, today's ENC is a church of about 350 people based on a collection of networks. Along the way, the challenge of sustainability has led them to radical re-thinks of how and where they operate.

ENC made history in 2009, being granted the Church of England's first Bishop's Mission Order and saying that it gave them a 'mandate to be missional' through connectedness with the wider church. But they have worked hard to avoid unhelpful duplication - rather than multiplication - in their networks. It's a challenge to keep the missional focus but the church's trajectory is to see what God is doing in Exeter and join in.

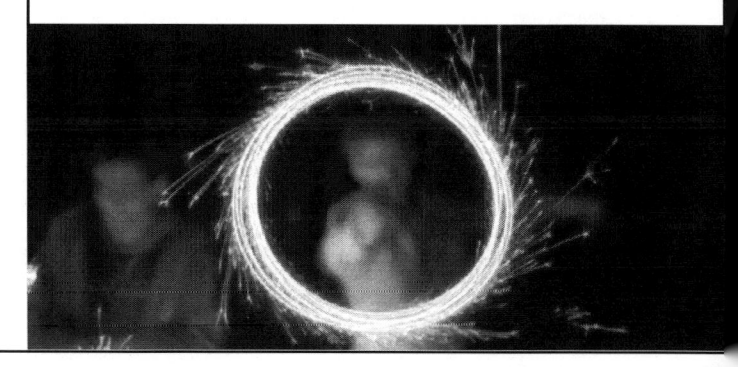

Shaped for the context

From the earliest days, founders of church should be asking, 'What sort of venture would be sustainable in this context?' Becoming sustainable begins with the intention to be sustainable.

How do you measure up?

This will raise issues of size and leadership. What size of venture is appropriate in this context? In particular, what size of venture is appropriate for the leadership gifts that are likely to be available?

It may be significant that the early church was based on the home. This meant that each household church was formed around an existing structure of leadership - the head of the family. Where in your context are the existing leaders, and what might church look like if it was built round them?

Being contextual is especially vital in relation to financial sustainability. Good questions to ask early on might include:
- what are the financial resources of the people we are called to serve?
- what sized initiative could they realistically sustain?
- for how long will the initial funding be available and is replacement funding from outside likely?
- what resources can the wider body of Christ realistically contribute, and for how long?

Handing over leadership

This is one of the most difficult decisions to contemplate. Who will be there when it is time for you to hand over the reins - and what is the best way for it to happen?

Who's next in line?

Working sustainably means thinking about transitioning from first to second generation leaders. A good mindset is to remember that the project is 'with' not 'for' the people the venture serves. So when will they be able to take ownership of it and run it?

When should you transition? About a century ago the missionary, Roland Allen, argued that missionaries should allow their converts to stand on their own feet as soon as possible.

He pointed out that St Paul rarely stayed with his new congregations for more than six months. Missionaries, he claimed, should move on rapidly in a similar way, relying not on their continued presence to sustain the new community, but on Scripture and the Holy Spirit.

> *expressions: making a difference*
> Fresh Expressions, 2011
> Chapter 13: re:generation
>
> re:generation has a deliberate policy of identifying emerging leaders.

> Roland Allen
> *Missionary Methods - St Paul's or Ours?*
> Lutterworth, 2006, ch8-10

There is an opposing view. Time and again, Paul left his new churches quickly because of local opposition rather than through choice (e.g. Acts 13.50; Acts 14.5-6, 20; Acts 17.5-10, Acts 13-14). Indeed, after being driven out of Thessalonica, Paul became highly anxious about the fate of his fledgling church there (1 Thessalonians 1.17-2.5). He seems to have worried that he had had to leave too soon.

In Corinth and Ephesus, where he had greater freedom, he stayed for over 18 months and three years respectively. Leaving new churches very quickly does not seem to have been Paul's intentional strategy.

Moving on rapidly may have been easier for Paul than it is sometimes for us. Paul's churches seem to have been built around converts from the local synagogue, where Paul typically started his missionary work (Acts 14.1).

These Jews and 'God-fearing Gentiles' knew their Scriptures - our Old Testament - well (Acts 17.11). So, appointing leaders from among them may not have been as much of a challenge as it is in some circumstances today, when new believers may have virtually no Biblical knowledge.

Jesus provides an alternative model. His departure at the ascension left the disciples humanly responsible for the formation and expansion of the church. He intentionally delegated his leadership.

Those assuming responsibility were far from being the finished article. Matthew tells us that some of the 11 disciples (it could read 'many') still doubted (Acts 28.17). Yet Jesus did not allow these doubts to derail his delegation. Rather, he embedded the principle of handing over leadership in the very origins of the church.

However, unlike Allen's account of St Paul, Jesus did not exit after only a few months. His closest disciples spent some three years with him, day after day. This was mentoring of a highly intense kind.

If the Jesus picture emphasises the importance of proper formation before passing on leadership, Paul's experience - despite often being driven by necessity - suggests that in some situations the hand-over can be remarkably fast.

The two pictures qualify each other. Paul's warns against raising the bar of Christian maturity too high before handing over leadership. Jesus warns against being too optimistic about the time it will take church founders to accomplish their task. The timing of when to move on requires discernment in context.

How might you discern? When they left, both Jesus and Paul left behind:

- **the Holy Spirit;**
- **a basic understanding of the gospel;**
- **the Old Testament - the equivalent of our Bible;**
- **Leadership;**
- **baptism and Holy Communion;**
- **in Paul's case, ongoing support - he kept in touch through his letters and his network of co-workers.**

Might whether these are in place be some helpful criteria for deciding when to leave?

Risk is always the big worry. Pioneers and others understandably fear that things may go wrong if the pioneer leaves too early. But that was same problem that Paul faced - and things did go wrong! Think of the church in Corinth!

Leadership involves learning by experience, including mistakes. Mistakes are the price of allowing new Christians to grow in their leadership gifts. It is a real price, but the gain is greater maturity and human flourishing.

Managing other transitions. Like most organisations, as a fresh expression starts and grows there will be times when it faces the challenge of making - for it - a significant transition.

One simple model suggests that the process of adaptive change involves three stages; 'initial organising' as a new venture develops, then 'mounting tension' as problems arise and finally a 'new emerging configuration' as solutions are found.

Dealing with problems

It is vital to know what to do when your fresh expression encounters inevitable stumbling blocks along the way. Going back to basics as to what you're doing and why will help to steer the venture back on course.

Challenge of change

When difficult problems arise, it helps to:

- **go back to your fundamental values;**

  'What are we about?' 'What are we trying to achieve?'

  This allows you to focus on the wood rather than the trees.

- **agree the principles that will guide how these values are expressed;**

  A cell-based church intending to grow further cells might agree four principles: each cell will have a mission focus, they will meet at least three times a month, their leaders will meet regularly in an accountability group and the cells will cluster together once a month.

- **allow maximum flexibility within these principles.**

  This freedom permits individuals to be creative within a framework that serves the venture's purpose, and this releases energy and generates fresh thinking.

Such an approach gives expression to Paul's vision in Romans 12 and 1 Corinthians 12 of shared ministry within the body, and reflects something of the way that Christ exercises servant leadership within the kingdom.

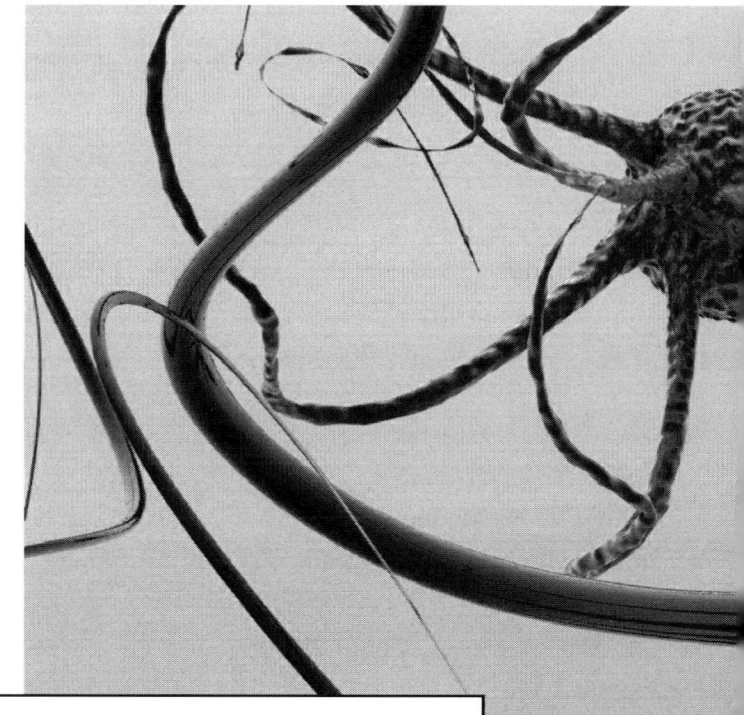

---

expressions: making a difference
Fresh Expressions, 2011
Chapter 23: The Sunday Sanctuary

DVD

The Sunday Sanctuary leaders are open to their fresh expression changing and evolving.

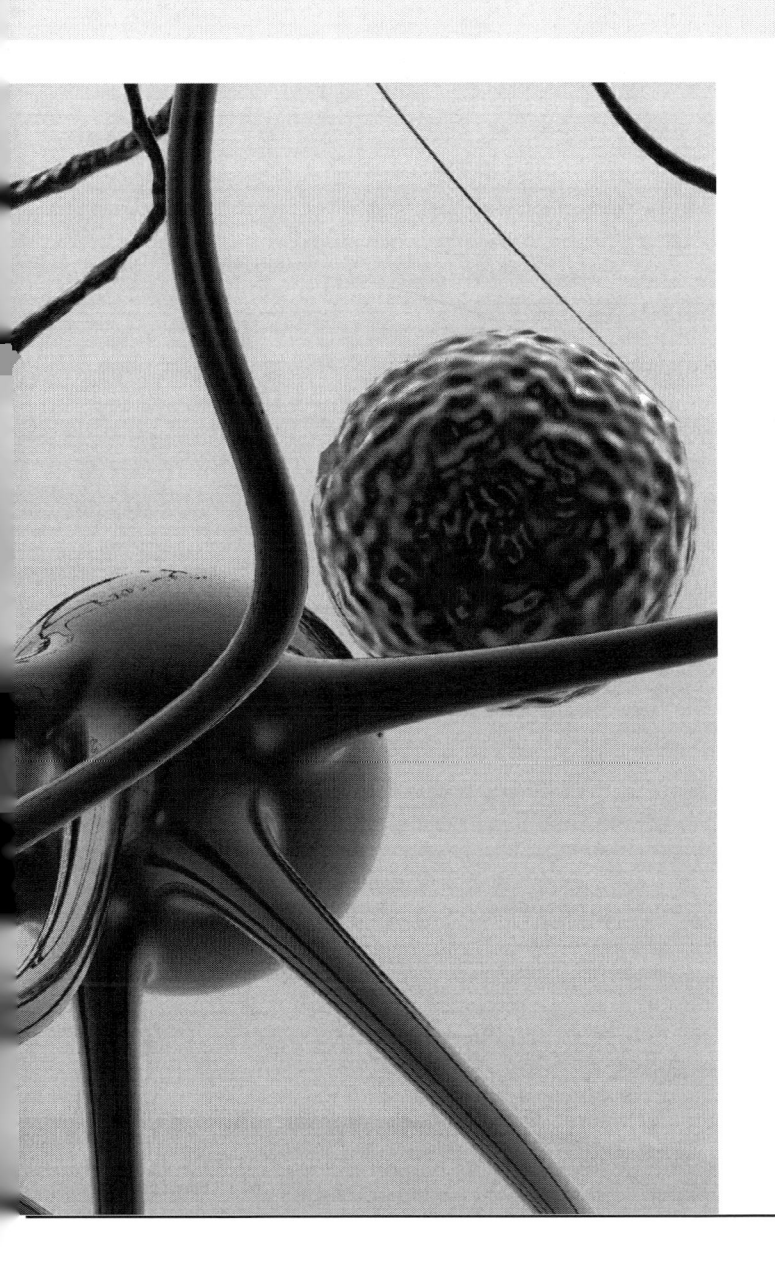

Some fresh expressions will need to become more strategic in their approach, as they get established and bear fruit. In the early days they could 'make it up as they went along' because they were discovering what would work in their setting. But having become established, they not only know what works for them, but they may also have become part of the local landscape, with links into the community and to other networks and churches.

Their experience, knowledge and connections with other people may mean that the situation feels not so totally out of their control. Depending on their size, they may be able to exert a certain amount of influence on their context. Instead of being at the mercy of events, to a small extent they may be in a position to shape local events.

All this may require different types of leadership and different forms of leadership structure. This is not really a shift from pioneering to pastoral leadership, which unhelpfully polarises the two. Pioneers need to pastor and pastors need to encourage innovation. The transition is more about an increased level of organisational complexity and the need for a greater emphasis on strategic thinking at the expense of ad hoc improvisation.

New skills may be required within the fresh expression to manage this transition and lead the church into the next phase of its life. Recognising that the venture has reached this stage is the first step to managing the transition effectively.

Grafted

Story

As a Church-Army-backed project in the Scottish borders, Grafted is based in the small village of Newcastleton but its work reaches much further afield.

They see their role as giving hope to those without hope and setting up and doing things that reflect the value of the church by 'being' rather than 'doing'. A drop-in centre at Hawick offers discipleship through its willingness to serve people and give genuine help to anyone who walks through the door.

Grafted works against the church's historic stance of demanding very high benchmarks of academic achievement for leadership, insisting that a lot of its work is as an onlooker to what the Holy Spirit is doing in growing the most unlikely of leaders.

The development of Refresh Community Church is one of the fruits of that work. About three quarters of the people who come are non-Christians with some 60 people from the community involved in one way or another. The aim of Refresh - comprising eight groups - is to encourage the development of missional people. As a result, church that's missional has become the norm' rather than an aspiration. It is something that has taken time to evolve.

At one point, a lot of people attending were Christians who wanted things to become more settled and comfortable. It was becoming a problem. The leadership went back to their fundamental values and responded by saying that, although Refresh worked well with traditional church in the area, they were called to be a mission group in the village. Their vision of Refresh was to be a lifeboat and resist the temptation to be a 'cruise liner'.

Some of those at Refresh are still involved with their local church and they did come close to meeting on a Sunday because of a desire to reach families but decided that wasn't the right way forward.

In the future, leaders hope that Refresh will continue to be guided by the very people that have come through their work at grass roots level.

Keeping the venture fresh

Running low on energy is a very real possibility after the adrenaline associated with establishing something new has gone. What can be done to ensure that your fresh expression has sufficient fuel to remain an effective force when initial excitement subsides?

Against the tide

There is a well-known process by which organisations become institutionalised. A leader with an inspirational vision forms a community, which stabilises in the second generation and formalises criteria for membership. In subsequent generations, much of the energy goes in maintaining and protecting established structures to ensure the community continues. Can fresh expressions avoid following this pattern?

Theologian John Drane identifies these temptations as a venture starts and grows:

- **a concern for efficiency**, such as replicating a model that has worked elsewhere - it seems quick and easy;
- **a trend toward calculability**, as demands grow to see numerical results;
- **a desire for predictability** - conformity to some pattern or other, perhaps inherited forms of worship;
- **a desire to retain some form of control** by existing churches.

He suggests four values that can work in the opposite direction:

- **creativity** as opposed to efficiency;
- **relationality** instead of calculability;
- **flexibility** (or adaptability) rather than predictability;
- **proactivity** - straining forward instead of holding on to the past - in place of control.

So how can these four counter-values become the heartbeat of a fresh expression? Milestone reviews, suggested in *Share+ How can we find our way? (Share booklet 05)*, offer one way.

Continuous review, which is central to the milestones approach, allows flexibility by making it easy to change course as necessary, flexibility will encourage creativity, involving people in the review process will promote relationality, while the looking forward aspect will foster proactivity.

> John Drane, *Resisting McDonaldization: fresh expressions of church for a new millennium*
> in Dave Male (editor)
> *Pioneers4Life: Explorations in theology and wisdom for pioneering leaders*
> BRF, 2011

> Michael Moynagh, Andy Freeman
> *Share: How can we find our way* (05)
> Fresh Expressions, 2011

Identifying fruitfulness is an important aspect of sustainability. It is a means of discerning where and how the Spirit is at work. It allows the question to be asked, as should be asked of an inherited church, whether a fresh expression is a fruitful or barren branch of the vine (John 15.1ff).

You might ask: In what ways are members of the venture growing in:

- **their relationships with God?**
- **serving people outside the venture?**
- **deeper fellowship?**
- **commitment to the wider body of Christ?**

Fruitfulness will be at the heart of a sustainable fresh expression, whether the venture is long-lasting or not. That is why we can prayerfully hope that as the Spirit works among us, fruit will be produced that endures and can be shared with others.

Sorted

Story

Keeping the venture fresh is at the heart of Sorted's work in Bradford. Church Army evangelist, and keen skateboader, Andy Milne started it in 2004 after getting to know the area's young skaters, many of whom went on to become founder members of the youth church.

Relationships were initially built through skateboarding but it's quite a small part of the Sorted 'package' now. They meet three times a week, seeing an average of 100 young people during that time. A Monday youth congregation, attracting 13 to 20-year-olds, gets involved in everything from setting up equipment to worship, teaching and prayer.

Tuesday nights are more discipleship-focused with five groups each led by two young people. Andy encourages them, saying that when they get involved in leadership it really helps their understanding. As they run it themselves, they 'own' it and the energy triples. Fridays see them have a testimony, short talk and different activities. The young people usually come through their friends or schools to these sessions because the Friday slot is very open and accessible. They get to know people and when there is a bit more trust they tend to move into the other two groups.

Some local churches realised they hadn't got the resources to do anything similar themselves but felt they could practically support something that's Kingdom work by allowing Sorted to use their buildings.

Sorted 2 was launched because organisers realised that about 80% of those in Sorted 1 were from the same 1200-pupil school. It is now running in the area's second school, the sixth largest secondary in the country with 1800 students.

A Church Army team now oversees the entire project. People from local churches also act as adult volunteers for each Sorted, this makes a tremendous difference because the schools' work is growing all the time.

This flexibility and proactivity in approach has also seen Sorted be granted a Bishop's Mission Order because it was noted at diocesan level that Sorted is not a seedbed for something else or an extension to another church. It's a church in its own right.

Published 2011 by Fresh Expressions
Registered charity #1080103

Copyright © Fresh Expressions 2011
freshexpressions.org.uk

Fresh Expressions, Athena Drive,
Tachbrook Park, Warwick, CV34 6RQ
0300 365 0563

Authors: Michael Moynagh, Andy Freeman
Series Editor: Karen Carter
Series Designer: Ben Clymo

freshexpressions.org.uk/share/booklets

ISBN 978-0-9568123-6-0

fresh expressions

Related resources

expressions: making a difference
(Fresh Expressions, 2011)

A DVD containing 28 stories illustrating the lessons to be learnt as fresh expressions of church make a difference to people's lives.

Available from
freshexpressions.org.uk/shop

sharetheguide.org

An online resource including a guide to fresh expressions, community, blog and learning networks.

freshexpressions.org.uk

Further stories and information, plus audio and video material and resources to download and purchase.